MIRRORED SOULS

Edited by

Natalie Nightingale

First published in Great Britain in 2002 by
POETRY NOW
Remus House,
Coltsfoot Drive,
Peterborough, PE2 9JX
Telephone (01733) 898101
Fax (01733) 313524

HB ISBN 0 75434 341 3
SB ISBN 0 75434 342 1

FOREWORD

Although we are a nation of poets we are accused of not reading poetry, or buying poetry books. After many years of listening to the incessant gripes of poetry publishers, I can only assume that the books they publish, in general, are books that most people do not want to read.

Poetry should not be obscure, introverted, and as cryptic as a crossword puzzle: it is the poet's duty to reach out and embrace the world.

The world owes the poet nothing and we should not be expected to dig and delve into a rambling discourse searching for some inner meaning.

The reason we write poetry (and almost all of us do) is because we want to communicate: an ideal; an idea; or a specific feeling.

Poetry is as essential in communication, as a letter; a radio; a telephone, and the main criterion for selecting the poems in this anthology is very simple: they communicate.

CONTENTS

THE PIANO PLAYER

His body sways with the emotional tide of music,
That aimlessly flows through fingertips,
Gentle fingers that make sounds so soft,
As soft as ripples on the water's edge,
Sometimes fingers pounce down on those keyboards,
Sounding so wild and dramatic,
There might as well be nobody else in the room,
Only himself and I,
My mind travels over distant hills,
Dreaming on top of a tide of music,
So high up that clouds are below me,
Eyes closed as the emotions that the music of Chopin,
Beethoven, Brahms,
Where should such beauty end,
But with the final note,
A wonderful spell has been broken,
As I raise my hands to applaud.

Angela Johnson

WINTER TURNING SPRING

In my heart it was deep winter, hibernating
Cold and in suspension.
The sudden thaw of autumn's freeze warmed my blood, my soul;
But it was fools' summer.
No sooner budded than withered,
Dreams dreamed and hopes half-hidden
Waiting for your sunshine
Faded, nipped and abruptly fallen
In frost-rimed death-dark depths.

But, chill-silvered, I turned,
Yearning for warmth and gilded
In the strength of the new season's sun.
Stem yielding, I wove toward the fresh source of dreams,
Whose need to dream too became itself a burning.
An innocent heat melded together undreamed-of harmonies
Created forests of thought and distances of stars,
Made fresh and brilliant
Winter turning spring.

Polly Larner

THE COLOUR OF NIGHT

My lady is fashioned from moonbeams
Turned on the lathe of the stars,
Shining through my dark hours
Like a bright lantern.

But silver is the colour
Of night and shadows
And the loneliness of purity:
The shade of fearful dreams
Conceived with a shiver.

The dark corners are
Without light,
So impenetrable and adamantine
In their blackness
That I quail from them.

And I have tried to grasp the moonlight,
Gather the quicksilver
Until, at the dawn,
I am left with nothing
But the gold of the fairies,
The silver of ashes,
The empty road to death.

Ted Harriott

SURVIVAL OF SORTS

I even found myself watching a programme
about baboons,
Which interest me little more than
Drying paint.
I needed to focus
But without soul-searching
Aloneness.
And so me and the baboons
Pondered my latest dilemma
In all its 'thou-shalt-not-fall-in-love-
With-someone-carrying-emotional-baggage'
Complexity.
How long do you wait for someone
To let go of their past?
Why were we not born with a genetic
'Switching-off' facility?
I'd sacrifice my 'need to understand' mind
For that of 'eat-drink-f***-forage',
Baboon style.
Sadly I'm not quite the missing link today,
And as the baboons are banged up
For medical research
With no room to move,
Or think. Trapped.
All too close for comfort
Methinks.

Jo Forbes

A HANDFUL OF SONGS

The Mountains of Mourne
Gortnamona and Phil The Fluter's Ball
Might never have been sung at all
If Percy French, student civil engineer,
Had not written Abdul Abulbul Amir
Sold his first piece and got smitten
By the need to follow his dream.

Captured by beauty of Irish countryside
While surveying bog land in Co Cavan
He gave in to his inner voice
And made his choice.
Phil The Fluter's Ball
And Slattery's Mounted Fut
Saw the light of day
And Civil Engineering
Went the way of family ambition.

Before long was a landscape painter
In Dublin city ran a witty comic paper
Later wrote two light operas
And one popular song followed another.
He made his name and had a mind to go
Across the sea to entertain.
Now rests in peace in Formby.

Freda Grieve

Come Times Of Poverty

We have decided to save our epics for our
later days and teach our family the ways
of expression that even God can't pause to listen
to and let his comments be known to all
of us we also find it hard to meet our costs
in particular our pensions that do not meet
with our cost of living demands.
We again find a lack of support from our local council
who are hoping to change one thousand pounds
to replace our front fence, now old and paintless
maybe just maybe our Lord in Heaven will
send us a token or two towards our offensive
fence in the front of our lovely house and just
maybe our poems collect to laugh in early times
of pension years so that so many will wither
away the dismal years in peace and memories. John X

J Richards

ETERNITY

He looked through the mirror
Stepped through it
Behind the waterfall lay sacred
A naked virgin sleeping
She was chained to a rock
Embraced in her hand a golden ring
Scribed on it 'free me someone'
He stood looking, a tear fell from his eye
He heard a cry of mercy
What shall he do, leave her now?
She'll die
A sound of freedom in his mind raging
Rebounding off the rock tomb
Hollowed in this cave stone room
'Awaken child, tell me your name'
Mercy she cries
A steel shackle cutting into her vein
'I'm the child of eternal youth
Sacrificed to the rain god
Take my hand, take this ring of eternity
My Saviour, set me free'
He opened his eyes, and saw the child within
Her name, 'Eternity'.

N Donaldson

THE WEAKEST LINK LADY

She stands there at the podium,
poised, forbidding, stark in black,
contrasted only by the 'auburn' hair
and, seemingly without a care,
commences her verbal attack.

Voice is honed to critical pitch,
eyes glaringly pierce thro' glass,
relentless without any nervous blink
barks questions - makes contestants 'shrink',
nervously say not 'bank' but 'pass'.

Between the rounds she 'follows-through',
intense, aggressive, forcing fears
unheeding, ever sure contestants 'stung',
asperity snapping from her acid tongue -
infrequently a smile appears.

Stark in black she stands aloof,
poised, arrogant in her stance,
glowering darkly yet with secret smirk
she cunningly performs her work,
executes well each hurtful chance.

'Tis show there at the podium,
stagecraft, illusion, stark in black,
survival only for the *strongest* link,
(at programme's end one sees her wink) -
'haradan' whizz of answer-back!

Ann Voaden

A BIRD'S EGG

On the beach you played alone.
In the garden you scattered stones.
Once - you were so near - we called,
but you did not seem to hear.
Perhaps this sense was not too keen?
But the truth was something other. Unforeseen.

You ride your bike, jump,
turn summersaults, spill the earth in the
plant pots, open and close cupboards,
slam doors, play the tape again and
again in the video.
But speaking? No.

You feed yourself quite happily. Succeed
in opening boxes and tearing wrappers.
It is *we* who feel unneeded.
Then, I heard how Freud said
autism is like a bird's egg.

A thin speckled shell,
blending in with the background.
You look fragile from the outside but then,
so does the moon in the clear morning sky.
You could easily survive
without the feathered insulation your parent provides.
The nourishment you need is also there inside.

One day, when you are ready
(a day which starts like any other)
you will hatch.
Peck through your air sac
fill your lungs, breathe for yourself.
Call for your mother.

Neil Halliday

RAINDROPS

Fall asleep
My little child
Dream of me
Never cry
For I have gone away
Where sun shines
My heart never cries.

Helen Owen

DEAD END KIDS

The early morning light
Awakes like a drawn curtain
My camera,
My face,
Among so many faces
Of the street.
I follow that newsreel
Of events down
To the bomb scares
That number nine bus
Out in the square
While pandemonium
Sets in round the terrace
To graffiti written walls.

Roger Thornton

The Cosmic Constant

My mind the universe,
An unknown quantity,
A vast unchartered shore,
With bright lights - darkened rooms.
Myriad of myths and harbingers of doom,
Begging out for the big crunch.
But the dark matter pushes further apart,
Gravity pressurises the planets of pain and pleasure.
Asteroids attack throwing dust clouds into my eyes,
Quantum chaos rules the waves and digs the graves.
A neurological nightmare of immense proportion
Rocks the very foundation of my basis of belief.
There is no cosmic cushion.
I recede further until there's only the horizon.
There's nothing left but this,
Lonely universe, lonely man.

Leslie Duggan

AURA OF AMBER

Caught in time amongst
the pendulum of thought,
Destiny with her delicate scales
carefully maintains the disguise,
from memories floating through
a reflection of the past.

Into the dark veins of emotion;
a momentary lapse,
a glance broke the camouflage
of a ghostly façade.

One faint sting of reality,
broken by whispers of perception.
Mystified by inner grace,
serenity enveloped the depths,
of her blurred vision
and fog-like feelings,
which cleared into a lilac mist
and shadowed her eternal soul.

Nicki Kilbey

FUTURE

There is no way I can see,
What is ahead of me.
Will it be happiness or sadness?
Maybe a bit of both.
I'll just have to make the most.
As does everybody in their life.
It's to look at what's gone on,
And wait for what's to come.
That is all that can be done.
If your life is in tatters,
Make what you have best.
Perhaps the strain of being rich would
Become better,
If you had a little less.
No matter what you are,
How much you are worth.
I say from when you are born,
Live each day the best that you can.
Don't mope about and let life get you down.
'Cause you don't know,
How long you will be around.

Richard James Ford (Deceased)

City Of Sea Shells

The water's edge of the evening sea
what raw power, roaring like a plane
with waves crashing with futile fury
onto the proud face of Worm's Head.
The sinking sun finally breaks free
from leaden clouds strangling the sky
and cloaking the cliffs looming high above.
It paints part of the iridescent sea
orange together with the silver and brown.

The bloody body of a lamb is lapped
by the indifferent sea, another victim
of this beautiful but merciless place
reminding me of the brutality of nature
as the gulls and sheep render a requiem.
I can see the wreck of the Helvetia
whose bones are covered daily by the sea
but by me lies another wreck hidden away.

The few tourists have gone as darkness comes
making everything sinister and the howling wind
I imagine to be tormented sailors' ghosts.
The seagulls are perched in the cliffs' crevices
under the ancient tide-blackened rocks.
The rising tide buries the unfortunate lamb,
everything is as mutable and as damned
as my city of seashells in the sand.

Guy Fletcher

THE LIGHT OF THE WORLD

Can you not hear Me?
Are you so obsessed with this world's racket?
Closed doors, closed windows, hearts closed to Me.
The noise of television's doubtful packet
Soaps and quizzes, violence to see
And then the bombs
When will you listen?
Don't you hear the knocking?

Why won't you hear Me?
Are you afraid of me? Why, why is that?
I came to you not so long ago,
Spread my arms, welcomed you back. You did not flee
But tried to detain Me, pinned Me to a tree
And then the tomb.
I heard the knocking
Nails in broken flesh.

Can you not see Me?
You passed Me yesterday drug-addled mind
'Help Me' I cried. But you hurried on your way
Put up the shutters, would not give me time
Yet I'll continue, will not go away
Maintain the bond
Still keep on knocking
Each and every day.

K Dry

THE LONESOME ROAD

Menace stalks the lonesome road,
Long shadows reaching out.
Tall trees their branches twisting,
Their shadows cast about.

No friendly light to show the way,
No soul to take one's hand.
Footsteps echoing, loud and strange,
Yet no one walks this land.

The hurrying traveller looks about,
Rasping breath tortured and hurt.
Nervous jumping at every sound
All senses keen and alert.

Terror prowls that lonesome road,
In sinister cloak of black.
Traveller, stay ahead of that dark clothe
Once enfolded you never come back.

Terrified on the lonesome road.
Rushes the traveller through the night.
Only the courage of an honest heart,
Can lead him into light.

Do not seek the lonesome road
For if you do, you may find
The signposts for that lonesome road
Are in your heart and your mind.

June Birchall

NEGLECT

She'd gone.
We went to check the house.

We found it had its own paced life -

An abstract sun shape on the table,
The pigeons, unstartled,
Cooing on the balcony

The hot hearts
Of the brown tinged cut roses.

Luxurious neglect, later to be rank.

An over-ripe Eden
Just after the Fall,
Still growing from tended roots.

We left, silently.
It was not our place to interfere.

Rebecca Reynolds

THE LAVATORY LADIES

Here in the subterranean gloom, like caring gnomes,
They dwelt in palaces of shining tiles and
Sumptuous marble: the Lavatory ladies.

Whilst we, like visitors to Dis, descended endless steps of
Diamond pitted stone, and clutched at banisters of ancient
Brass, cleaned by their loving hands.

Here these good ladies greeted us with gracious smiles
And quickened steps to flush the gleaming china
Bowl, and wipe the seat with expert flip,
That no outrageous sight or smell disturb our sanguined bliss.

How posh we felt when we bestowed a silver coin and not the
Mandatory Penny. How puffed with pride to leave our
Hard-earned cash on surreptitious plates. How dignified their
Taking of our patronizing gift. They would remember us when
Nature called us once again to enter their domain.

Yet we in turn must play our part, and sympathise or tut
Upon their ills, and those of sons and daughters;
Whilst all around the banging doors proclaimed the
Exodus of Clientele indifferent to their needs.

They will not die this noble breed, though Time has
Swept away the marble and the brass; yet still
They wait upon our pleasure with scented aerosol, and
Fluffy toys, whilst all the day the thunderous dryers
Blast our hands with deafening roar, and lowered
Ghetto blasters cackle on.

No vandal, junkie, or graffiti art shall quell their Dunkirk hearts.
Long may they reign to bring relief to all who seek their
Hallowed halls; the Lavatory Ladies of England.

Margaret Carl Hibbs

STILL LIFE

A thought of yesteryear,
Like an animal which harbours psychic activity,
Distant, yet profound in dream.
A small flower,
Gentle, yet harsh,
The sense of touch,
Colour so vibrant,
A stamen, a scent,
The reality of life.
A celebration of the known,
But not the contemplated.

L A Evans

EMOTIONS

A bird
Silent in flight
Gliding on the current
Stretching its wings to maximum
Pure *joy.*

Eyes spark
Thick eyebrows drawn
Preparing to explode
Not caring who or what is hurt
Anger.

A dream
A sweet young girl
Dressed in gossamer white
Floating gently up to heaven
Love is.

Wilhelmina Cobb

A LITTLE IMAGINATION

Waving trees abstract shapes
To my eyes.
Imagination of moving animals
Blown by wind underneath
Bright skies.
Shape of an elephant a lioness
A bear.
Me to look around see if there
Are other shapes to imagine there?
When you are whiling away a little
Time having a bit of your own space,
Have you ever on a blue-sky day
With puffy white clouds visualised
Something in cloud shape riding our sky
In space.
We do see definite distinctive shapes
As we look around.
But it can be fun to let your old
Imagination run as you can see things
So natural in asemblance they you astound.
There is time for positiveness
Time for visualisation fun.
No cares no worries no harm is done.

Victoria Joan Theedam

SOLACE

In the comfort of the heavens
Asleep inside an angel's soft wing
In the light of the moon's watchful eye
I feel I belong
Inside this night-time solace
As the star sky brightly reveals
My destiny
In a sparkle code of secrets
I read angel whispers
With each deep heartbeat
Their breath is so warm
In the cold darkness of reality
I feel safe
And this oblivion
Becomes my best friend forever . . .

Louise Lucas

POSTCARDS FROM HEAVEN

Look for the beauty around us,
patience is a flower that grows,
not in everyone's garden.
The scent of a rose that I love,
recalling happy memories,
the laughter and the tears.
Lighting up our faithful hearts,
I think of you,
and how things used to be,
I'll keep in my heart,
for I remember you.

Smile and you will see,
that everyone will be friendly to you.
A friendly wave you sometimes get.
it's so nice from one whom you respect.
Just imagine how it makes one feel,
a lovely sight quite often seen,
you will soon have lots of friends,
that pleasant smile and easy manner.

We are often touched by the
Tenderness of others.
What is it all about? because
I don't know all the answers,
I am a stranger here myself.
My mysterious guardian angel,
took command of my life entirely.

Genowefa A Ziarko

MEDITATION

Were I to search I would not find
A bay as wide as this,
Misty and grey
Just as today.
It lends a transient bliss,
An altered consciousness
That makes me to lie down
Upon this restive strand
Of pebble, wetted sand.

Far to the west a streak of gold,
A sunset's roseate form,
Prismatic light,
Refracted, bright,
Yet from the dark deep's born
Wild horses of a storm.
My thoughts I now place down
On bleached and polished stone
To savour peace alone.

The clouds may part, the stars appear
To weakly pulse and fade,
The moon when full
Pale as spun wool,
Its radiant orb displayed,
Mysterious its façade.
But greater is God's light
Upon whose path are sent
Pilgrims and penitents.

Frances M Searle

KESWICK

We stroll by the lake.
The patchwork quilt of greens and soft browns
rise up as rounded hills,
their feet dipping into the sheet of cool water, still and reflective.
Threadlike paths criss-cross the slopes.
Resembling moving dots, distant sheep and hikers
aim for a place above the clouds.
Haze and mists wipe out part of the hills
mystically blurring their contours.
After evening rain the smell of the earth rises from
burrowing moles sweeping the soil into rounded miniature mounds.
The evergreens show glossy leaves as though nature has polished them
to outshine their deciduous neighbours.
Only the copper lustre of scattered fallen beech leaves
hint of the vibrant colour left from the previous year.
On graceful larches, lichened bark with wisps of pale green
cotton wool,
mimic the gossamer tents of spiders' webs lacing the damp grass.
The delicate woven threads spotted with droplets of transparent light
hide the elusive spider waiting for its innocent prey.
Yellow celandine and white wood anemones dot the undergrowth
where ferns uncurl their patterned fronds toward splinters of light
that force their way between the trees.
Nature unfolds as we move towards Friar's Crag.
There we sit gazing over Derwentwater,
reflecting and digesting its beauty.

Audrey Faulkner O'Connor

Santa Eulalia Del Rio, Ibiza

Beyond the windows the sunshine explodes.
Square houses call in virgin joy across
The clear blue waters to the clear blue sky.
Their whiteness fills the air everywhere.
Tall maize creates a haze swaying above
Rivered red soil to where pink bay roses
Shade the chairs and tables while taut strings strum
Cool drinks away. Into the mind boldly
Pass bosoms of brown girls whose movements lithe
Are captured in never fading snapshots
In the filing system of Time, notes of
Music for future reference in that
Other clime. These moments, dancing crystals,
Cascade, with golden beaches, silver roads,
Fishing barques and dark-eyed rogues, sparkling in
Streams into the wine glass of memory.

Desmond Tarrant

DANCIN' IN THE HAGUE

Dark and smoky
saxophone sobbin'
lip smackin'
North Sea stompin'
Jazz Fest.

Cool slides down the scale
notes newly born
sing out through the night
'cross the Plein.
The Hague sways
with the blues.

Heads shakin'
tails snakin'
listen to the man.
Dr John's healin' touch
cleans the night.

Beer sippin'
grass smokin'
chillin' with the crowd.
Eyes meetin'
bodies touchin'
hot slides down the scale.

Rona Laycock

LIFE

Born again
You cry your first cry, you're a newborn babe
In the comfort of your mother's arms
Boy or girl the feeling's the same,
The comfort, the warmth it's all the same.
You'll learn to walk and talk run play and fight
Eventually you'll grow above your parents in height.

You remember you were ten, then twenty and thirty and more
Those once bright eyes have dulled once more
You grow older and older
Wise beyond your years
As you get older you long for a younger person's eyes, and ears.

As funny as it seems now, no one really knows
Why when we are young, we long to be old and age
Is it possible that it's because of all the fun adults get up to?
Like shopping, paying the bills and an occasional vindaloo,
Or is it something else only known to you and me . . ?

Life is such a precious thing that many of us abuse
Through drinks or drugs and even suicide, to name but a few.
You see I've seen the things of terror
And faced death head on many times
I've seen parents of a loved one crying
Because of drugs and alcohol abuse, even suicide.

So why do we do this, why cause so much pain?
To me life is precious and to you, it should be the same.
It doesn't matter what your friends
Tell you or what other people say . . . Life is precious
From the moment it's born to the end of a single day . . .

Michael Lee Gooch

SIREN'S SONG

Lately
marker buoys appear as Sirens
depicting dangerous currents
dwelling beneath a point of view.

Learning to float
is a prerequisite to swimming.
Recognising signals allow early
warnings of treacherous motions.

Ballast
an adjustment of necessity -
a perfect balance
the objective.

Watch out
for hidden rocks. Lie on your back
but stay your course. Don't let
the waves overwhelm you.

Tranquillity
comes to those who close their ears
to Siren's song and search for depth
behind alluring sparkling facades.

Edward L Smith & Carmen M Pursifull

SEA-STRAIN

As a child you fought the sea -
Between surf and sand, rainbowed in salty spray
(The geometry of spots and stripes on costume, bucket, spade
A happy, fearsome talisman) you'd build defences;
Engineer deep ditches, high blockades,
Order seashell armies into ranks
Impenetrable-seeming, and there,
Kings of castles, fly defiant flags!

What were you afraid of? Had you
Come upon wrecks like bones,
Bodies tempest-tossed and broken;
Glimpsed monsters, where the mind
Sharks in the sleep-dark deep,
Where tendrils trawl and drag depth-down?
Did dark ship up some hideous birth
To engulf, fall, swell, drown?

Of course you could not win. Soon enough
Wet fingers would poke holes into your keep;
Then with buckle, break, suck and gush
See stronghold fold with hungry kiss!
Stain and strain; waves delicately unfurled
Atom by atom your embryonic world.

Let salt water dissolve castles made of sand.
Of myself I give you to plant at the world's last strand.

Donna Triggs

TONIGHT

The familiar bed prodded her
Tired limbs. Tonight was no different

Reading poetry in inadequate light.
Though the lines consoled, they tore
Her heart. Ritualised grief it was,
Taller than her life. Like the bedclothes,
Words that tangled, heavy as a weapon.

She cracked the spine of the book
By long habit, folding down a wide corner
Of the aching page. Sleep composed itself
Like the words still
Printed on her lips.

Robert James Berry

THE HILL

The climb was steep,
The path hard to follow,
But in one's mind we knew the way,
It grew harder as time went by,
Voices and sounds began to dim,
Hands clasped hands, and held on tight,
No more worries or cares,
Are we there? You know you are,
The place, a name,
We know from afar,
'Tis . . . Heaven.

William A B Mennie

KISMET

Flaming fiery orb
Searing the soul.
Molten heat glowing,
Scorching sand,
Gehenna.
Parched throat
Screaming silently.
Burning eyes scan
The nebulous horizon's
Shimmering haze.
Black vultures hover,
Harpies from Hell,
Pitiless.
Frail hope fades
Tortured I seek oblivion
Come for me Abaddon.

Margaret Ball

HER RUBY RING

Ruby and diamonds flew
into her room
From mystery stars
and a magical moon.

Her diamonds were wishes
and dreams untold
To bring smiles from a frown
and warmth from the cold.

Her ruby, a kiss
'neath a magical moon
Love 'o' love by two
And the mystery stars
lit the way in the night
As wishes and kiss
they flew.

Janet Munnings

MUSIC THROUGH WATER

Attracted by such sound
I brush aside branches, crush ferns
oblivious of thorns that pierce my skin.
I breathe in moist grass,
tornadoes of sound
drag me from the woodland path
to come upon sheer cliff
perpendicular rough rock,
striated layers which show
their change through time.
In furious force waters
cascade in sparkling spray.
Cacophony of sound
a deep bass thrum of drums
swells diminishes in high chord
as flood becomes a trickle.

Sonorous violins
counterpoint in sequence
of soft trills from flute
to bell tones of glockenspiel
froth and foam detonate
on rock. A stream snakes down,
winds to eventual rest
in hidden depths.

I plunge my hand, searching
through concentric rings and pluck
wet pebbles, black, smooth and small,
to shine on rare memory,
to roll wet inside my palm.

Elizabeth A Hackman

INTERCEDING SPIRIT

Cloistered in his study, scanning his unfinished sermon -
Freezing from the Arctic breeze screeching through the common -
The parson jerked from his reverie by taps at his window,
By a frail damsel, convulsed and covered with flakes of snow!
'Who art thou, and what ails thee at this hour, my little maid?'
Queried the parson, pointing to the door, and walked ahead;
Said she, incoherently, 'My dad is dying of cancer,
And pleads that, to him, the Last Rites thou must administer.'
Recognising her as the daughter of a parishioner.
The parson hesitatingly agreed to go with her:

The night was dark - the path slosh, so a lantern they did take,
To light them through the snow, right up to the very cottage.
An astonished, fatigued lady answered the door, trembling -
'Padre, How did you know that my dear husband was dying?'
Replied the parson, 'It is your daughter who brought me here!'
Then, looked he for the damsel, who vanished into thin air!
'Can't be,' said mum, 'Ruth died in an accident years ago -'
'Who was it then that escorted me to your very door?'
They stared vacantly at each other, inane and nonplussed.

Sacrament dispensed, the ailing man died. Divinely blessed.
Baffled by this mysterious girl, the parson remembered
Some workmen doing roadwork, he had earlier encountered:
Returning by the self-same route, he stopped to question them;
'Mates, did you not see two of us walk past you with a lantern?'
'No parson, we saw you *alone* - but talking to yourself,
And we wondered whether you were drunk, or beside yourself!'

It was Ruth's spirit - the parson knew it, that very instant -
Who, sans flesh and bones, was his interceding visitant!
Next day, *Sunday*, his sermon was not the one he prepared,
But a testimony on the nocti-encounter he had . . .

Welch Jeyaraj Balasingam

ATTITUDES

I think with one owning the right attitude of trying
to solve a row, is commendable.
I also think you see we get the wrong attitude
plus the right attitude, and in the pursuit of
our daily living.
So I think in that context, the qualities of us
and in possession of the correct attitude is paramount
and no less I feel the benefits of the right attitude is enormous
and a wrong attitude likely to be a disaster.
Here then, is my contribution to your place who
kindly made your offers, and as my introduction.

James Callaghan

MODERN FAMILY

My brother went mad when I was twenty-one
My sister fought my father and tore me apart
Dead wasps in a jam jar in a dull Dutch town
Bored by the pain in my dad's dying heart
How can you build a life on foundations of rock
When you're afloat on an ocean of fate's ill luck?
Things don't make sense, the pieces don't fit
But I still need a plan to make the best of it.
Emotions are for people, not places and things,
The people that hurt me are now wasps without wings
Original sin takes abuse too far,
Take me as I am, like I love you like you are.
It's the roller coaster of a modern family,
But, my African wife, I've learned to trust thee.

J Dean

GUSTS WELCOME

Seeing this small castle, in the quiet of Wales,
On the board outside was a little sign.
This is a haunted castle.

Come and see inside
We went inside and it really was so spooky,
The rooms were really large and nearly empty.
With candles everywhere. Some had fallen over,
The wood fire smelled of rose wood.
A tape was very quiet and spooky.

We just stood,
We looked in all the corners, to see what we could find,
Both wires and batteries everywhere.
The doors would creak, the rooms were large and spooky.
They led through the place, even in the garden.
Although there was little space . . .

There were no ghosts
But man-made noise in everything.
People really believed it, but
What happened if there was a power cut?

Heather Ann Breadnam

WHITBY GRAVEYARD

We tottered
up one hundred steps,
to gaze at the skyline
of terracotta gravestones,
blackened by the breath
of the sea. On the way
down, we espied a
sprite, chasing a soapy
wave, until the foam
was washed clean
away. The blanket
of water had kept the
waiting sand warm,
but we chose hot
pebbles instead to
massage our aching feet.

C Karalius

THE WORKERS

The working man,
May appear dull,
To the superior, lofty, intellectual.
But,
Amongst these seemingly,
Drab and dull individuals,
There are those
Who write poems of beauty,
Which would astound some,
Who,
In such cultured tones,
Dismiss them,
As merely drones.

John Troughton

POETRY
(Written after reading a collection of poetry by Spike Milligan)

Some is as a nicely woven cloth.
In some there is more than a glimpse of soul.
Whilst others delineate fault lines in another's life.

Come take my hand and lead me through
an opening crack in the many dimensions of reality.
Approached in fear and glimpsed through tears.

In jest, we may at best, dimly see
the unspeakable beyond our reach.
If before the fading daylight leaches
even that, poetry can seize within its grasp
and make manifest some mystery then,
Just as in an acorn can be an oak.
In an inkbottle we can find the world.

Jack Major

PRIVATE MOMENT

He stood, like a monument to modern man
on the sand hill turf
Red beard, red hair mussed by the breeze
Blue eyes, gold rimmed specs
Striped shorts, thongs
T-shirt labelled 'Billabong'

Not there to swim or surf
Observe the wind and setting sun
fling rose and ochre scarves
across an opal sky
Motionless, beside the throbbing sea

Strapped to his breast
a canvas carry-cot
With dark-haired infant, calm in sleep

The father could not turn his gaze elsewhere
Oblivious to walkers, talkers,
romping dogs, my covert stare
Gently stroked soft cheeks
with roughened fingers
Touched tenderly the downy head
Love, like an anthem, flowed between

Did he dream of future years
See indeed the child, the man
Or simply marvel at the charms
inherent in this blossom from his seed?

A precious, private moment
Somehow shared
by every man who ever held
a cherished newborn in his arms.

Betty Hocking

BLUE EYES

The young man
Went off to war
With a song
In his heart

A load of care
Looking over his shoulder
The smoke filled the sky
His eyes looked blue
He wanted to cry
When out of the mist
His friend walked by
With a song
In his heart and
A tear in his eye

Helen Owen

OLD WOMAN

I look in the mirror, and what do I see?
A face full of lines, yes that's me!
But each line tells a story of births,
Happiness and sheer hell! And many more
Things, who can tell? My eyes tell of
Hopes, and dreams that didn't come true.
I am sure reader, this fits some of you.
Now I've reached my three score and ten,
Even though I'd live it all over again,
But next time would be different
Whatever the cost, trying much harder
To make hopes and dreams come true
Because as you see, in the end
It's all up to you.

E Clarke

THE CORMORANT

On mudflats pointing
Towards the sea
The Cormorant stands
In majesty.
His territory
His land
Washed by the
Ocean's mighty hand.

Maureen Oglesby

THE TRAMP

The tramp goes on his way
Not a care in the world
People stop and stare
That doesn't bother him
What made him go like that
No one will ever know
Looking in bins
for something to eat
Bottles and cans are empty
nothing to drink
Then somebody threw
him a coin
At last I can get something
to eat and drink
Before I face the fields
and stars for my bed.

E Bevans

SLEEPY TIME FOR SLEEPY HEAD

Sleepy time for sleepy head
Rest awhile and drift upon my shoulder
Or lay back at peace easing into the pillow.
Surrender,
Stretch out your mind
The soft, creeping glow of
A restful sleep.
Drifting you away into a
Satisfied peace
Soothing your worries and letting
Your dreams awaken.

Jennifer Cook

RECOLLECTION

I have seen a fly die
Naturally, at ease,
Stretching out its long legs,
Once bunched for flight.
It breathed once, then lay
At full length an instant,
'Thanks' it said,
Then reposefully
Laid its long length to rest.

Beatrice V Gwynn

PARADISE KINGDOM

I met a man as good as I am
And many more there must be for sure

If you want to live in paradise kid
Be kind to animals, that's where they live

And you will have a life just as nice as the animals
No sin or vice, they deserve their paradise

Michael Norman Darvill

THAT DEMON CALLED PAIN

It causes so many people grief and strife, children so
young and man and wife. The more one tries to ignore it
the worse it becomes. The Demon Pain affects us all,
from builders, postmen, priests and nuns.

It insinuates one's quiet moments, tearing through the
nerves. Wake up, I am back, no rest for you today.
All the pills in the world won't make me go away.
One fights the Demon Pain through all our learning curves.

Rest this way, stretch and bend, heat treatment,
electric shocks. Ah, it's on the mend. Bliss for a while,
then oh no, the Demon's back again.

'Fooled you that time,' says he, that Demon Pain.
We try once more to boot him out through the door,
but now that Demon Pain, has declared all out war.
It fights us in the head, it fights us all the more, hips,
backs, arms and in the leg.

We shed tears of rage, to our doctor we beg,
'Please make it go away, that Demon Pain.'
Our doctors do the best they can to help us on our way,
but we all know that Demon Pain won't stay away.
Each generation, sod's law, it's there again.

Kathleen Collins

OUR UNIVERSE

Our world is in an atmosphere
Of nothingness
The wonder of it all
How can we begin to explain
But we believe in the nature of it all
And we are on it for a purpose

J Campbell-Jones

LIKE THE SUN

The sun shines by itself way up in the sky
I let my light shine by and by
For certain people
But most of the time
Like the sun, I'm alone

It can be difficult
Living without another human being
As the people I talk to are
Existing
Not living at all

They look but can't see
They listen but cannot hear
They walk but go nowhere

And so like the sun in the sky
I'm forced
To play *Solitaire*

Noel Lawler

DEPRESSION

It's odd how things occur in normal folk.
Mimic the sick, becoming manic in order to cope
Sort out all the problems in one day or night,
Taking action, or taking flight.

Over the years, I've noticed that
A little smile, a little chat
Makes us happier by far,
Than drinking in the nearest bar;
Drowning our sorrows for an hour
Feeling we've regained our power.
The benefit is short,
It doesn't work, it doesn't stick,
Floating away again so very quick.

Incensed with fear and doubt
Rented hollow, wanting to shout.

Taking actions, don't stop, don't think,
Not having time to even blink,
Rush and push and phone and call
Molesting one and all.

When exhausted, start to slip
Into a dark unhealthy trip
Don't get up and make the bed,
Evil thoughts are in our head.
Swinging up and down we go.
Feel scared, unloved and we don't know,
What to do, what to say,
How to look forward to a brighter day.

Sheila Ann Pashley

MEXICAN NIGHTS

I feel your pulse closer to me,
I taste every salty part of you.
If this is love, I lust in wait,
For an embrace of inevitable fate
I cannot avoid this want so deep
Where your feminine parts may weep.
I know in time, a kiss will bring
With you Mexican nights with sleep.
My sensuous, divine and living girl
How can you keep me far,
Where each day and night you touch my world
And your glow my ambient star.

Anthony Rosato

LONGING

To see you
To hear you
To feel you as the breeze blows over you
Am I to rejoice no more?
My soul and spirit
To be elated no more
Because I am in your presence?
Oh please let time
And fortune from above
Bring me again
To you my greatest love
Ancient and wonderful
Bodmin Moor

Marda

WHERE WERE YOU DADDY?

Where were you Daddy when the world began?
Where were you Daddy when they introduced man,
To temptation and strife, and man took a wife,
Where were you Daddy?

Where were you Daddy when man spread his seed?
Where were you Daddy when man had the need,
To conquer the Earth for what it was worth,
Where were you Daddy?

Where were you Daddy when they introduced law?
Where were you Daddy when man went to war,
To fight with his might for the things that were right,
Where were you Daddy?

Where were you Daddy when man came back maimed?
Where were you Daddy when the politicians claimed,
The sacrifice of men justifies the end,
Where were you Daddy?

Where were you Daddy when The Depression came?
Where were you Daddy when man felt the shame,
Of not being able to provide food for the table,
Where were you Daddy?

Where were you Daddy when I came on the scene?
Where was I Daddy, where had I been,
Whilst man was evolving, and the world's problems solving,
Where was I Daddy?

Alun Harries

WRITER'S BLOCK

(To all poets everywhere)

It's no good: I can't write.
No inspiration: Little concentration.
Plenty of perspiration: Oodles of frustration.
101 Dalmatians: No! That's not right.
Cross it out.

It's no good: I still can't write.
Can't think; can't sleep; can't eat; can't drink.
No. That's not true: I must be at the desperate stage,
When anything looks good on an empty page.
Cross it out.

It's still no good: I just can't write.
I'll be sitting here again all night!
It's true I'm telling you: The more I try the less I do.
'Dear Mister Heller, Re-Catch 22'.
Cross it out!

Kick words about, scream and shout,
What do I want to write about?
I haven't a syntactically poetic clue.
I'll wager, Mister Wordsworth, it was the same for you,
Coleridge, Keats and Shelley, too.

Now, wait a bit! I've had an idea.
The fog is lifting: My mind is clear.
Why struggle with flowers, mariners and birds,
When I could rhyme a verse in the genre absurd?

I shall compose a piece about the shock
Of a writer having a writer's block.
Yes. That's it.
Done.

Carole Wale

DREAM CATCHER

Dream catcher, dream catcher
Please capture my dreams
Cast them down into silver streams
Let them flow to an ocean wide
To dance again on the morning tide.

Dream catcher, dream catcher
Please eclipse my dreams
Bind them with some soft moonbeams
Take my dreams to the heavens high
And mix them with the midnight sky.

Dream catcher, dream catcher
Please cherish my dreams
Nurture them by whatever means
Hold them near, don't let them stray
I may need them for another day.

George S Johnstone

THE STATUE

A garden long forgotten and overgrown
Hides a ruin where once had been,
An ancient house of majesty
A Lord and Lady's dream.

And in a bed of nettles there she lay,
Her once proud body,
White and warmed by the summer sun
Now green with earth's cold, damp decay.

Remembering how her time begun
With fond hands moulding her in clay,
As though she a queen of stately grace
With Grecian hair and fair of face.

Is that a tear on her lovely cheek
Or just the rain in sad respect,
Telling her of one who cares
To see her lying in neglect.

Ada Ferguson

THE PASSING OF THE YEARS

O let me go thou terror of the night
With dreams of what I might have done
Though it's nice to think as oft I do
Of days of youthful exuberance
Of friends alike with aims like you
And days fulfilled if given the chance
I have been a ploughman
I have been a pigman
What strength remaineth for what I can?
I have been a carter
With geldings and mares
I have been a thresher of oats and tares
I have been a farmer with all its cares
I look at my toil worn hands
And the veins standing out like horns of rams
As nature grows robust and covers the lands
So what remaineth, for what I can?
I worry in my dreams of fright
A weakling, now not very bright
And fear that I might lose my sight
For what remaineth, for what I can?
The restless nights of dreams so clear
The fruitless efforts which cost me dear
I cannot remember an empty day
I cannot think what more to say
Now can I go, what can I do?
O let me go thou terror of the night.

Fred Simpson

THE OP AND AFTERWARDS CANCER WARD, MUNICH

A spinal incision sent me to sleep
    but no visions
hoped for or deep-down feared,
    merely a green world the next day
and shadows and the constant bleep

of electronics, a kind of Leicester Square
    with green lights; healers not whores
here; now a shallow sea
    where your wide-eyed vagueness floated
waiting for denizens like me to rise for air.

And later the beings in white, wings
    folded, trolley-wielding,
harrying sloth, healers in a hive
    keeping their charges going with in-depth stings,

forced exercise and white lies.
    This species delays decay for peanuts,
throw-outs, promises rarely kept -
    the only angels between us and our demise.

R G Bishop

In Other Words

They were there
In other words . . .
Being at home *(sweet home)*

They were going there
In other words . . .
'Have a nice time y'all'
'Gee thanks - we'll surely try' *(smiles)*

They went there
In other words . . .
Fighting thru the goddamn traffic
Nearly missed the goddamn plane *(goddamn it)*

They were going there
In other words . . .
'Ladies and gentlemen, this is your captain speaking'
'On behalf of American Airlines - welcome aboard' *(Sit! Stay!)*

They were there
In other words . . .
Who is that guy?
What is going on?
Why is he doing that? *(Everything's changed)*

They were going there
In other words . . .
Being hijacked *(Oh no! Oh shit! Oh no!)*

They did not go there
They did not go there
They were there
In other words
Operation Infinite Justice *(They are not anywhere)*
(They are everywhere)

Linda Sisson

STARLIGHTS

Across a high, purple dome,
The clouds set sail for home.
And I on a cafe terrace
Could not know
When, why or where the swallows had flown.
Night, and the city lights outshone
The mass of smaller stars above,
But a few blinking souls stood out, in love
With the soft wind's flow,
And clinking cups below.
Still I could not know
Just when the soft, new shoots had grown
Or when and if the swallow's flown.
Lit, dim red cigarettes;
Can it be that we are free to fret,
Or take in a wasteful whim
And wantonly forget?
No hand alone can hold
Regular hot, frappuccino cold:
Passion or cautious reason
Can fashion regrets
In shifting seasons.
Still, ashy mounds and coffee grounds
And red-rimmed cups are but
Conditions of the lease.
And never did I know
How, or when or where
The swallows disappear
In flights beyond the cappuccinos.
Somehow it's hard to comprehend
Capistrano
Or the end.

Benjamin Tyree

ON FIRST VISITING SCILLY

Islands in the sun
Sparkling sea
The call of a bird in flight
All this, and me!

Flowers of every hue
Shimmering sky
Sand and shells
And here am I.

Choppy sea
Whipping spray
Screaming gulls
Another day.

Boats chugging
Ropes tied
Wind whistling
Low tide.

Gentle breezes, daffodils
Ripples on the shore
My soul refreshed
It yearns no more.

Alison Watkins

LIGHT

Light is might, and sorely stressed,
A mother no longer holds baby to breast,
The sound wave so elusive, bathed in secrecy,
Senseless murder of millions,
Too young, to feel the attendant death.

Babies in their cradles weep,
And who can see the sound wave steep,
Loud, the death knell tries to keep,
Live from the womb to dispel sleep.

And all must mourn,
The passing of the deep,
Eternal love.

Jean Bald

MOONSTRUCK MARINER

O nymph of the night, come -
My feelings to tease
To drive me wild and my senses please
My mysterious maiden of charm.
With soft music floating
On the sigh of a breeze
My arms want to hold you close
But I dare not blink lest you fade away
My heart you have captured
I beg you to stay.
So don't mind if I stand
No offence if I stare
Bewitched by the night and the moon in your hair
A delicate prism of moonbeams so bright
Did you ride to Earth on a star?
Could the sail of my ship be seen way up high?
Could it be just for me that to Earth you did fly?
My sail is set, I'm adventure bound
Will you come and sail with me?
We will ride the wake of a shooting star
Sail through the night, no matter how far
And voyage the seas of the sky together.

Olga Johnson

THE DARK

I feared the dark as a child
And if I had to go upstairs alone
I'd make sure all the lights were on first
If a shadow came wandering past
I'd jump out of my skin and scream
Whatever it may be
I'd fear there would be something hiding
Among my bed sheets,
Under the bed,
Or even behind the curtain
I never have been one for the dark
And I still fear it at sixteen.

Laura Perkins

OLD LIBRARY BOOKS
(Old, damaged library books are removed from circulation)

Cradling the restless at bedtime or beguiling
The bored on Sunday afternoons,
Filling the hungry with good things
And giving the fretful
Something new to play with;
Lying between neat covers on bed tables,
Or openly dishevelled on a sofa,
Itchy with biscuit crumbs, stained
By a splash of tea, a smear of chocolate,
And passed promiscuous from hand to hand

They now, having attained a certain age
And looking frankly knocked about a bit,
Spine going, pages past repair,
Will find themselves, being no longer viable,
No longer even
On the shelf.

Valerie Perring

RED, RED FOREVER RED, RED

Red roses, the thorns dripping bloody blood, red, red, red
Smell the aroma of success, sweet success
Stiletto thorns, stiletto sharp bayonets

Heaven on the threshold of Hell
One step away from Heaven, one step too close to Hell
Red roses, the thorns dripping bloody blood, red, red, red

An angel, a banshee
Bewitching Lord, yes I, Yes I, Yes I
Stiletto thorns, stiletto sharp bayonets

Whispering words of passion and tenderness
Consume the fire of Heaven and Hell
Red roses, the thorns dripping bloody blood, red, red, red

Lord have mercy, pray silently Lord, Yes, I Yes, I
Is she an angel or a banshee bewitching Lord, Yes I
Stiletto thorns, stiletto sharp bayonets

So near to ecstasy, one step closer to Hell
Air conditioned Heaven. Centrally heated Hell
Red rose, the thorns dripping bloody blood, red, red, red
Stiletto thorns, stiletto sharp bayonets.

Lorand Tabith

WISDOM

Knowledge is born
    in the curiosity
    of a child.

Peeping, prying, snooping,
    why, where, how drives
    the desire to know.

Out of this desire
    to explain
    knowledge evolves.

Possession of knowledge
    does not assure
    wisdom.

Wisdom is a divine gift
    from ancient times
    given to a chosen few.

Mary Elaine Vanderwulp

THE TEMPTRESS

I stand alone, quietly
Musing on your tranquillity,
Ears closed to the strident
Chants from neon-lit pavements
Harsh and garish.

I stand alone, in silence,
Breathing in your fragrance,
I hear your gentle sigh
Soft as a mother's lullaby,
Soothing, calming.

I stand alone while gazing
At the Monet moon awaking,
Golden threads of appliqué
Sewn on silken negligée,
Wooing, seducing

Wavelets, curling
Sleepy arms around the shore,
Soft, enticing paramour,
Whispering in tempting tone,
I listen as I stand alone.

Margaret Brewster

SO-CALLED PATRIOTISM
(Does it really matter?)

Have you ever heard
the people who are proud of their nation?
It's just another form of discrimination.

My country is better than yours
so on and so forth,
does it really matter?

We are all the same
forget the language,
forget the colour
forget the faith,
life is more precious than that.

This so-called patriotism is a disease
it corrupts the minds of the people,
creating hatred among neighbours.

The borders between nations
don't really exist,
the sooner they fall
the better mankind will be.

Corwin Barber

AGAINST CYNICISM

When lunacy's in season,
And hate and greed,
All the more reason,
All the more need,
To spell out a creed
Of love and reason.

The bud concealed
Must come to flower;
Truth unrevealed
Can have no power;
Through lips unsealed
God has His hour.

Deborah Maccoby

THE LITTLE DARLINGS

The little darlings
Doing the things you just love
They think right
You think wrong
The little darlings.

The little darlings
Drawing on the walls,
Not on paper.
The terrible two's
The temper tantrums
The little darlings.

The little darlings
Some live up to their name.
Angels from their bones out.
The little darlings.

Oh the little darlings.

Emma Pearce

FOR A SAILOR

In a sunken submarine beneath the sea
Lay one hundred and eighteen men trying to get free
In sub zero temperature they gather around
Not a whisper, not a sound
Taking turns who's next to breathe
Beneath the frozen Bering Sea.

Up above the Arctic winds
The coldest ever been
Ships sail around but can't go down
To the men beneath the sea.

Mankind and the powers to be
None can control the sea
So take time out, a minute please
Say a prayer for those beneath the sea.

A McKenna

CHASING TIME

Why am I always chasing time, running after the hands of the clock
tick-tock, tick-tock?

It never gets me very far just back to square one.

The following day it's never 'hooray' . . .
It's, 'Oh no, look at the time.
I'm going to be late!
I have no time to meditate!'

And then I'll moan that 'Spirit' isn't coming very close,
how can I alleviate the course of events?

So once again I sit and ask 'Spirit'
and of course I receive the same as the last time.

Make time my friend to meditate.
Make time my friend to meet at the gate.

And look beneath and you will find
the grass of green that feels so kind.

And up above the sky of blue that gives the vibes that always soothes
and that feeling of tranquillity, that comes from 'Spirit' just for Thee.

You'll smell the fragrance of rose-pink flowers
and forget about those minutes and hours.

You'll hear the song of birds in trees
and receive those feelings that set you at ease.

And when you realise these feelings so sublime, so peaceful, so happy,
like an everlasting smile,
you'll hear the footsteps from the lane, nearing your domain.

And here they are all looking healthy, it's Uncle Bryn and Aunt Elsie,
and close behind it's Bob the dog with Gran and Gransh
and all the mob, who came to see me because I made the effort,
I'll tell you my friends, it's truly worth it!

After long conversations mixed with giggles and laughs and exchanges from all our pasts, it's time to come back to the hands of the clock, tick-tock, tick-tock.

But never mind my time will come when this journey I'm on will be finished and won, and then I will meet at the end of the lane another soul like me, feeling the same . . . tick-tock, tick-tock.

Geraldine Jones
4 years 8 months old from the world of spirit

THE GARDENER'S WIFE

She wanted passion.
He was busy on the allotment,
growing prize onions fit to burst
into orgasm,
a wonder to behold.
She, in her isolated boudoir,
sits dreaming, of a strong and forceful lover
caressing her neck with silken fingertips.
Bliss.
His onions won first prize,
months of caring, nurturing the seed
had come to fruition.
His photograph appeared in the local Gazette.
Her dreams lay shattered on the cold, hard ground.

Emelie Buckner

REFLECTIONS

Capture green, spongy hillocks soft to touch,
Where sea thrift nod to gentians and creeping stone crop,
In a cleft at Cliff Castle an Iron Age fort,
Such beauty discovered and 'peace' we had sought,
Below the green water caresses each boulder,
As sea birds swoop on their prey,
When a gentle thrum thrum of a small fishing boat echoes across
                                                    the bay,
Fishermen pull hand over hand heaving crab pots on deck,
A 'catch' disappointing to say the least,
Yet arduous tasks never cease.

Puffy, white clouds float under vivid, blue skies,
As pleasure boats cruise round 'The Mouls' rock,
Seagulls scatter amidst megaphone chatter tranquillity soon disappears,
As if to add to these bellowing voices,
A grey cloud looming also rejoices,
Then rain diagonally blown by the breeze creates a picture with
                                                    perfection and ease,
For each blade of grass becomes shimmering bright,
Each flower has petals of silk,
Pools on the pathway reflect the sun,
And puffy, white clouds have re-spun,
Rabbits romp under where pinnacles rise,
Lichen covered against late summer skies.

Hazel Sheppard

DEAD END JOB

Down at the local mortuary
At a gathering of stiffs
Anonymous, there is a very
Busy man.
He's busy plugging nostrils
And rectums and tying silk
Ribbons around flaccid penises.

He knows how important impressions
Are in his sensitive trade.
Women in particular pay great attention
To the smallest detail - so he has to be
Conscientious even in his dead end job.

Yet he can rest assured that the day
Will come when he no longer has this
Task to perform.
Down at the local mortuary stiffs anonymous
Will one day welcome him to their platform.

Alan Holdsworth

IS IT TOO LATE?

The world awakes to destruction
Too late or not too late?
That is the question.
From fields of richness,
Pollution - pours out death
On troubled water . . .

Be gone, oh cruel and heartless men
And leave the world,
To caring hearts and minds.
A city crumbles . . .
You have destroyed their hopes,
Of peace and understanding . . .

Oh country of sorrow - and
World of chattering teeth.
Beneath thy great walls
Their souls cry out -
For mercy - to the foe:
And nations weep . . .

Fear not - oh gentle people.
Thy faith is ever strong
You still believe.
Let not men of evil
Destroy thy very soul
Your day will come . . .

Born out of misery
Without justice or freedom.
Crushed by poverty and war,
It is not too late -
To rise again - and live . . .
In Peace.

Mary P Linney

THE STEAM PACKET NAMED UNCLE SAM

Upon a summer's day,
Came sailing along a funny steam packet,
Which was full of passengers and fine sailors making a racket,
All in cheerful mood and high spirits, they sang.

With so much clatter, singing, 'Hi Dilly Ho,'
It was an American steam packet named Uncle Sam,
Down the mighty Mississippi it would pass,
Stopping at every destination so fast.

That the music and gambling would never stop,
Until the captain sounded his great, big horn,
With three enormous hoots, ding-dong, ding-dong, ding-dong,
Which seemingly made all the clatter worst.

When one rich, old lady shouted through all the din,
'Oh, golly gosh, I do declare, what silly boat am I on?'
The first officer then replied, 'It's an American boat Ma'am.
You're in the United States of America, let me take your arm.'

'Oh, don't try to kid me son, I do know where I am,
It's just that, I'm a little bit confused right now.'
He then replied, 'Are you not English, Ma'am?'
'Why, officer, I might be drunk, but I'm not that dignified son.

Are you my husband, or am I losing my mind?'
'I don't know Ma'am,' he then replied.
This went on for about five or ten minutes more,
Until the officer exclaimed, 'No Madam, my name is Uncle Sam,

This here boat, is named after my dear daddy, Ma'am.'
'Why officer, it must be all this sweet champagne I've had.'
'Now come here dear lady, it's now getting far beyond a joke,
So let me escort you shore side awhile.'

'Hi Dilly Ho,' she replied.
'This boat is shore side officer, it's never been afloat.
Why, I do declare officer, this dream boat must be in Heaven.'
'No, Ma'am, it's down the Mississippi river,
Going to a port named Devon.'

James Cameron

A CHILDHOOD WISH

I had one wish
It was a big wish for me
I was three years old when it started for me
I wished upon the stars above
Please come and rescue us
From our pain and fear
Our cries of help which were plain and clear.
Why did nobody hear?
My wish was, get me out of here!
I would look out my window at night
To the stars, big and bright
'Please take us away to where you are'
One day like a bolt from the blue
My one wish came true.
The hurt and pain we suffered was taken away
Thank you stars above, my one wish had been heard at last!
No more pain, no more fear, no more suffering
At long last my wish was here.

Sharon Smith

MIND

Your mind is vast, an inspiration,
Echoing clear and bright,
Stories untold, paved with gold,
Volumes stored for life,
Mysterious, inviting, intriguing, exciting,
Wonderful times so rare,
Sealed in a vacuum, released in a moment,
Time to reflect and share.

Eileen Brown

CONFUSION

Confusion in my mind, in my heart, in my soul.
Twisted moments of reasoning, plagued by unclear thoughts.
My very being diminished and perturbed
By the very confusion that stems from within.

Confusion is all that anyone sees, confusion is a mystery to me.
I have tried to reason and stop my aching head,
Age has no bearing on what I have said.
Young or old, sane or not, that is the question, confusion.

Clarity is short, confusion controls,
Help break this cycle from my mind.
Twisted like wire around my brain,
Turned into the thoughts that remain.

Confusion, my existence, my future for now,
Look inside this inner shell.

No one can see the torment that's me
What is the point of explaining.
Confusion will remain all the same.

Sandra Johns

AMID THE FALLEN!

I wish to write,
But I know not, what I might;
As I'm steering into the darkness,
In an attempt to spot some light.
A light amid the confusion
Of what might be, the hidden solution.
But I would if I could,
Although I couldn't as I wouldn't;
Because the real reason still remains hidden!

Only because our world of worlds collided.
And in the explosion we became divided
Simply blown different ways amid the ricochet
Of the worlds we'd simply made.
Even though we've since come back together;
We're merely living in the shade,
Within the shade of one another!

Dave White

MEETING

I met a man in the street,
We are kindred souls
From different lands.
He is black,
I am white,
So different,
So alike.

Separated by thousands of miles
We met by chance
Here, where I was
Born, we are
Brother and sister,
Kindred souls.
He is black,
I am white,
So different,
So alike.

Barbara Zoppi

LAST ORDERS

My town is black and white this night
And the streets yawn back
Wet with boredom.

Spent up in every sense
The journey back seems longer
When it's raining.

Streetlights snake and break
Round black hole roads
Star systems on their own.

Past the old school now, through drizzle
And the cobbled alley of memory
To dirty your knees.

I spy with keen peepers of mine
Eyes that is to you
My beginning and end.

Walking home alone
Another Friday been and gone
Until the next one.

Liam Allan

A WILL

Why make a Will
When you don't feel ill?
I know it makes sense
But the very thought
Makes me feel tense.
I look around the things I've collected
Not much, you might say
But to me they are precious in every way
Will they be proud to display them
As I have done
Or hide them away, from the light and the sun?
But then I stop, and think
I won't know when I have to go
I can only state what I would like
And a Will will make it right
There's only one thing I can't leave in a Will
The love that I feel
But they know, they know.

B Green

NOMINAL FRIENDS

I saw her last on a station bench
    (one dark winter's dusk, at four)
She spent five years at the heart of the class
    while I sat it out by the door.

Made friends by the same initials
    and a curious middle name
We should perhaps have been partners
    as Sherwell and Silwood found fame.

Her train was late; so too my wife's
    we talked of that and this
We should perhaps have been lovers
    instead I left with a kiss.

Harold Wonham

DISTANCE LANDS

I'm standing in a field,
Surrounded by wild flowers
And ripening grass.

As I observe the biosphere,
The sun begins to shine.
A soft and gentle rainfall,
Descends upon the universe
Enriching all living organism.

There's a great rainbow coloured arc,
In the atmosphere.
For some strange reason
People stop and stare.

Like the four seasons.
Time is never, never still.

Upon this dampen earth,
There's a puddle, growing
Bigger and bigger with every
Tiny raindrop that falls upon
This universe.

Suddenly, that single puddle
Becomes a mirror, reflecting
My ancestors of long ago.

A single teardrop appears.
Unable to control my pent-up
Emotions any longer, I'm dreaming
Of my homeland.

Brian Ross

UNTITLED

I am now in my ninetieth year,
I like a pint of beer
But when I read the news
There is little, one can cheer.
Mugging of folk
To pay for their dope,
Elderly people, afraid to live alone
War all over the world
I am sorry, I do not want to moan
I will pop up, and have a pint
That will put me right.

John Knight

Duty, But It's Meant To Be Duty Free!

Something about Freud and psychotherapy:
as I am doing, explore one's fantasies,
letting go the logic of living,
taking my feelings very seriously,
this world can keep turning without me -
an image of my father, my childhood envy
but, as a child, what put me off my father!
A non-smoker by genes, who actually smoked.

To him, a cigarette, red-hot at one end,
fiddling with it between his fingers
to avoid a mischance of getting burnt -
whilst all my friends could smoke surreptitiously
hiding a fag in the curve of a hand - if a copper about!
Now, in advanced age I give thanks to Dad
for so inadvertently putting me off smoking
thus setting me up for a grand old age!

Jim Lucas

LIFE IS . . .

A drama each moment
with variety and tears,
a test of stretching sums
where noughts are lost!
A journey with too much baggage
and nothing to wear!
A precious second in time
with personal joy and fun,
a day of mishaps beyond belief
when the world seemed mad,
a pageant of excitement
and pantomimes for all the family!
A tedious business meeting
when nothing much is achieved,
a collision of strong wills
where faint hearts tremble,
a shopping trip in the rain
without a Mac or umbrella!
A meal with friends or barbecue in the garden,
a hairdresser appointment
when the trainee is let loose!
A mirror of temperaments
and creative miracles,
a torrent of surprises
where challenges are met,
a children's party
where all the balloons have lost air!
A fantasy or reality
the choice is yours!

Margaret Ann Wheatley

NOCTURNE

The distant sound of the last bus
Fades into a deep blue suburb.
An empty crisp packet floats
Upon an isolated puddle
Reflecting an intermittent
Shocking pink neon light.
Exhaust fumes linger in the
Desolate bus shelter,
Drifting and settling upon
A damp pavement.

The still fauna silently coughs
In sympathy with the compressed
Sound of solitary laughter
From the hotel foyer.
I turn from my window
To see the bedroom wall
Engulfed in moonlight.
I sit on the end of my bed
And fall headfirst into
Unconsciousness.

Neville Anthony

Affirmation

I will learn to be autonomous
To take responsibility for myself
In all my relationships and decisions
I will seek the truth in deed and word
In fact and feeling, in head and heart.

I will not allow myself to be manipulated
Especially by those whose creed is based
On greed, or in the mindless rape
Of this planet. Yet I will reach out
To my neighbour and not allow my help
Or friendship to be corrupted by those
Who would control all relationships
In the name of state, or ideology
Or profit or hate.

I will work to bring into existence
And to nurture a faith that life
On this planet can be joyful for all;
That we, humankind, must fully accept
Our responsibility as the dominant species,
Whilst humbly acknowledging that the
Laws of the universe apply equally to us.

The way will not be soft and smooth.
We each have a battleground within us.
We will gain insight and strength
By going forward together.

Margaret Chisman

MAKE ME A SMILE

With a simple story
A joke a rhyme
He makes me laugh
An amazing story unfolds

Girls - Boys - Men - Women
About them all
What happened
How it was
Just a rhyme
A joke
A simple story
Which made me
Smile.

E A Triggs

FRAGMENTS OF LIFE

Thoughtless deed
harsh and hasty
speech rung out in bitter tone
shattered a silent soul
words now disowned
made the first division.

Tracey Spencer

A NEW SUN BURNS

How quick the clock runs back,
How soon the tables turn.
When thinking that the winter's over,
And feasting with old foes,
You find that former friends
Have found a way
To make a new sun burn.

So swift the memory fades
Of decades in the race,
Rhetoric of bygone years forgot.
How fast the club expands
Engulfing even madder states.
The poor just wait
For some sign of God's face.

L K Clements

FRAGMENTED THOUGHTS

Fragmented thoughts -
Creating distance and space
Looking outside
To a world full of flowers and arched beams.

Sitting here
Somewhere inside your sanctuary
I become the observer and student of life
Full of rich, soft petals of lilies
And small, red lights
Reminding me of Valentine's Day
Lying somewhere within my gaze.

Through the magic of this new-found youth
You appear timeless
And I innocent and naïve
There seem to be no more tears to cry from lessons learnt
And my experiences before
Have been frozen and thrown into a capsule
Buried somewhere in my subconscious.

There is freedom in this metamorphosis
And I see change as opening up, returning to childhood
Where honesty and self expression
Are in their freest state;
Fluid water instead of crystallised ice.

Free thoughts,
Free wills,
Free spirits,
Free of blame
The only way I can visualise this instant
Would be a blue flash of colour
In butterflies wings.

Cinsia Wilde

WHISPERS

A whisper passes
By my ears
Almost silent
No one hears
A gentle sound
Among the trees
The whisper of
A summer breeze.

Colin Boynton

CONSIDERATE REMIX 2002

The spaces in-between are the most frightening
The subtler concepts I can't comprehend
I'm a bird in a cage and I'm flattered, but I still can't fly
There was never a soul to engage me, to sing me a lullaby.

So I'm disconnected, resurrected
Saying I'm alive when I'm dead again, twice over
There are metres I don't want to walk
Hills I don't want to climb, hard for me at times.

There's a place I can breathe and I need that room to grow
Manoeuvre my way round the big, dark centre, find myself within
The little boy I carry around
A somewhat tarnished item in the Lost & Found.

Andy Hinkinson-Hodnett

JAMES SAYS

'Writers Write!'
That's what they do!
He says in a smug way.
I write rubbish!

'Words on a page'
he says 'that's all it is!'
But why are his words
so good?

'Take your pen for a walk!'
He says. Why?
When my pen keeps reaching
a brick wall.

'If you can't see it or
hear it, don't do it,'
said twice for emphasis whilst wagging finger.
Screenplays; more like screen doors.

Jean K Washbourne

GIFT

Gratefully!
Eye pierces the
flower's beauty
imbibing its healing.
Simultaneously -
slaughtering - suffering,
Humanity
All where.
Evil prevails.

Sringkhala

PING PONG BALL

A world was leaving me,
shrunk to a ping pong ball
somewhere mid ocean.
I batted and watched it go
to nothing; birthdays bobbin
with Christmases, tinsel of
India's sun. Like the one
I tried to shut away -
baubles in a drawer
his words of English shores
to stave off the salt taste
of this sprayed beginning.
Drowning in new sounds
the time my father found me
in the empty auditorium.
They played for me alone;
staccato men in black and white,
my world in pitch and foam.
And I, back row,
ribbons, pigtails, swinging
to the rhythm, invisible
without a world.

Patricia Maubec

Briefly, age 10,
on the ship from
India to England,
I batted a ping pong ball
into the sea and
watched it bob away.
This was my world
leaving me!

Birth Of A Mosquito

It slipped out almost transparent
from invisible satin space,
beneath glassy water.

It reached with long proboscis,
beyond the day's quivering,
outlined by cascading colours:

Its vibrancy increased
like a Harrier jet charging its engine:

then, as if it remembered
it could breathe above water,
it shot out into space with a fulminating buzz,
that was soon part of an orchestrated hum.

R Fenech

DIVINITY

I believe I am divine
You may think my thinking perverse.
Fine thinking but reversed
But I have seen the signs.

It has not been a heavenly bolt
More a gentle realisation
Rather than a heavenly revelation
A gentle touch rather than a jolt.

I am not by sin untainted
The extract of barley and corn
I have never been known to scorn
But no sinner is as bad as painted.

On what base do I lay claim
Not some alteration of physic
Or some devious alteration non-specific
But a function in dictionary named.

Thus with truth I believe
I have with scientific fact discerned
Wine into water I have turned
When I pass water and myself relieve.

It may be a miracle of a piddling sort
But alcohol I have turned to water
Have I natural laws of science altered?
In passing I would like to say I am self taught.

Brian Norman

THIS IS NOT A PRAYER

Do not forgive me Lord
For I have sinned.
And do not forgive the others
For they will sin again.
It's not your place to forgive
In a world where you don't fit in.
You cannot forgive me, Lord;
Only I can,
From within.

Lydia Moore

I SHALL NEVER ABANDON YOU

(My menopause Lover)

As you sight with boredom on this endless evening,
When you weep and you wail over your still-born dreams,
Over all that you crave yet could never achieve,
And for your beauty gone, those alluviums of fat,
An old Thing, discarded for a younger model,
I will stand by you.
As you bear in silence, your heavy heart flaming,
The scolding tidal wave of another hot flush,
Scorned by the lost sunsets of your bygone moon tides,
Walled by fear, buried under
Layers upon layers of having your fingers burned,
I shall console you.
As you gag on the bitterness that comes from never feeling
The caress of a hand, the wetness of a kiss,
As your hair greys, your teeth decay, your bones brittle,
And you would rather starve than cook dinner for one,
I will smile at you.
As you smoke endless fags, riddled with athlete's foot,
Watching the Box all night so that you will not scream
Through your ancestral possessions, delusions, hallucinations,
I shall always witness you.
As you sob the failure that comes from not trying
And, defeated, aching, utter your silent curse:
'Why? How! I can't . . .'
I shall never abandon you.
Together, living ghosts, we will travel
To the land of your dreams.

Brigitte Ariel

AOTEARORA

Tell me, New Zealand, land of stained glass and fern
Why you chose for your symbol the kiwi.
Shy, night bound bird, unable to fly or impress,
Except for its egg, a near third its own size,
Unrivalled proportion, its sole claim to fame.

Your mountains, lakes, glaciers, rivers and fjords
All belie the calendar calm of a land
Where geysers, quakes, tremors and sulphurous pools
Attest the ominous rage of forces unseen.
Again why the kiwi? Innocuous thing.

Land of the Maoris, proud warrior people
And tough pioneers, now joined in the haka,
Dance of defiance and sporting machismo.
Nation of men, who fought far away wars,
Why brandish the kiwi, a timorous bird?

I ask why the kiwi, lacklustre creature,
Should somehow portray the radiant figures
Of Rutherford, Hilary, Mansfield, McCahon.
I search for the irony that might reveal
Why this inconspicuous bird is your sign.

Maybe, just maybe, that egg holds the answer.
On this scale the diffident kiwi's supreme.
And so a slight bird depicts a small nation
Where so very few have accomplished so much
In the legendary land of the long white cloud.

Rex Baker

TRAVERSE

When I look in the mirror what I see wavers unsteadily
I look in from without, avoid the dishes, then on with my shoes
These shoes, they take me anywhere I want to go, upon request

They take me to a wooded glade emblazoned by autumn sunshine
To a dingy house with the same old faces, the same obsessions
Pretending to like me, for they once knew my name! But no store

Do I set in being liked; if I am ugly then let it be so, if I am weird
In their stoned eyes, I'm even weirder in straighter eyes than theirs
And still fobbed off by those who care less for me than I for them

I'm weary of self-transmogrification, always altering for others
A smiling, nodding social register. I have these shoes upon my feet
Deep and timeless books upon my shelves, a mind sharp
                                        if a little twisted

I want for nothing more, I will want for nothing more. This day
I say this, and bequeath to myself what I should have years ago:
I will be me to the best of my ability, loyalty must be earned

By my friends, not dragged out to be shattered on the altar
Of egoism. Held close were all the rejections felt, words dispensed
With brevity and little thought for me, a capering sarcastic fool

I walk alone at night for many miles to lose the pain inside
Though it never goes, and the rain-sleeked paths lead ever on
To the rainbow settling snugly, obscured in wishful thorny ground

Blood-letting ground, smattered with the tears of the ancients
We seek elusive threads to bear the insidious sensations
Described in the air in traced-back acid moments; time stops

The reflection is in the mind not the water, and it stares back
It always stares back, for there are some places even we are scared
To traverse within our own minds. You'd better get your shoes on.

M Keirle

ALL IN THE MIND?

Just the eye
Of a window
Looked
Across
At me.
For I was just
The other side
Instead of being
Within.
Two worlds
Completely
Different.
Yet both
One and the same.
Just a different
Perspective.
And that
Is the name
Of
The
Game.

Lyn Sandford

TEARDROP

Makes all the difference.
Leaf's single tear
Resting near
The edge of an abyss.

Reflecting grey expanse
Amidst a sea of green.
Falls softly in between

Time and space.
Ripples to displace

Two million hopeful dreams.

Sarah Boyes

ON BOARD A KETCH

The thick blanket of darkness
Has engulfed both land and sea.
As I toss sleepless on my bunk
I hear an orchestra warm up!

Lashing rain plays pianoforte
While the rigging takes up the violin
Screeching and moaning out of tune.
The boom in protest whines and cries
So then the anchor chain joins in
Banging the symbols, crash, crash, *bang.*

The wind being conductor then takes charge
With halyard goes tap, tap, tap,
Whirling baton thus sets the pace,
Calling all instruments to order.

First the boat creakily obeys
Slowing down from its heavy rock
Until the music's rhythm flows
And then, to blissful sleep!

Pamela Gillies

THE DIG

The arcs of their axes branch the horizon,
in well plucked frown lines across the brow of the earth.
They work with a fever.
Spatula hands furrow, expectant, tremble over findings
with the sensitivity of willow.
They question whether it will be gold,
fear the caustic humour of the soil.

Edward Long Shanks stands over six foot,
splaying his presence deep into the ground in oaky roots.
Below him the world crouches like a toad,
staring at his coarse hair bleached yellow with urine.

His femur lies askance,
pointing away from his body laid out like tooth picks.
If the girl straddled above him pouts her lips,
blows once more at the loose soil,
she will find the gnarled head of the bone,
protruding from the earth like ivory ginger.

Long Shanks settles back into the granite pew,
making a nave with the length of his lower body,
grinding the gritty mud in his fingers like poppy seeds.
He yawns. His mouth gapes open like a lion,
the fat of a goose hanging from the corners of his mouth like slobber.
He roars with laughter.

The girl prepares to wake him
She wears the axe in her hair,
tucked behind her ear like a frozen stem or rhino tusk.

Bobbing their heads up like rabbits,
the diggers hang on her eyes,
watch small handfuls of dust break away from the bone,
revealing more bone, a square of red cloth, and finally a skull.

Long Shanks is poorly dressed for his visitors,
has not the eyes to warn them,
nor the larynx intact to express his anger.

Melanie Challenger

ENGLAND'S RESURRECTION

The Dawn of England's sweet Virgin-Rose
Did to England bring, long defiled in darkness deposed
The healing Graceful Light of England's Tudor-Rose
That casting out the Papal-Norman Yoke
Restored England's long dead hope.

And so in this bright Occidental-Star was love, much reposed
And from our Virgin-Star ascendant
Did healing balm from Edward days
Upon us bathe resplendent.

Yet on foreign shore
From his arrogance-ness, Paul-Four
A writ did issue forth
That from healing balm
It did recoil in fear and terror
And didst proclaim an Angli-Kin error
And in arrogance-vile, demanded that:

'Lest renounce, we, our Virgin-Queen,
Admit she be-naught but whore.
And come she to the Court of Paul-Four
Where on her knees, she will fall,
And in mercy-beg, she will crawl.

Then . . .

The Horsemen Four and Burning Stake will land
On England's Green and Pleasant Land.'

Geoff Shoun

THE BELL

. . . Round one.
As the bell rings the crowd begin to sing.

Warriors step forward in all their gleaming glory
The eyes lock, and do take stock, the depth of each's fury
Crash, clash, bone and flesh, they wish to smash.
A dart, a dash, their leathered arms do flash.

A strike, a blow, how far? How long? to go . . .

The thinker's mind does click and turn,
The warrior's heart begins to burn.

A breath, to breathe, with their bodies they dance, they weave.

An inferno, a living hell, who can do so well?
. . . final round.
With an echoing ring there is the final bell.

Gary De'Roux

CLIPPED WINGS

I clean your crooked hands,
Held broken birds
Stiff and strong,
Full of life that does not fit
A hand's story.
What do they do
These restless flightless things?
Where do their bones begin and end?
Pitched in the point of my back
Where my clipped wings start.
Your hands twitch
As I clean them
And I feel my amputated flight.
Fenced in with glittering rings
Time thickened and real.
If I was to turn around
I would have to look again
In your spotted mirror
And realise how broken I am.
With phantom wings
And broken fences
And restless hands.

Julia Burns

SIGHT WITHOUT LIGHT

Do not grieve because you think I cannot see.
My eyes may not light, but I have sight
Reaching far beyond your confined horizons.
The sun can always shine, each day be fine.
My world is not limited by my vision
As long as my mind's eye does not die.

Feel not sorry because my ways are not yours
I see so much with merely a touch.
Your voice can tell me a lot more than your look.
A voice can hide what is meant inside.
I can reach beyond the superficial you
I see your heart, the important part.

I am not sad because you label me blind.
My world no less bright through lack of sight.
I just have to listen more for warning bells.
Reading my books with fingers, not looks.
Be not afraid to offer aid when needed
Like you I need help to get me through.

I am a normal human being with my white stick.
I only have a different point of view, from you.

Polly Bennison

In Sadness I Am

Search for me in the shadows,
And you'll see me in your fears,
I am the face in the clouds,
And the sparkle in your tears.

You'll know me in your sorrow,
I am the bite in your pain,
I am the nothing in the hollow,
I am confusion in your brain.

Feel me brush you as the wind blows,
The gentle kisses of the rain,
The emotions that your heart shows,
The hesitation in refrain.

I'm the relief of the breath you draw,
The swelling of your heart,
I am the why in the what for,
And the go in the start.

I am the only distance,
I am the pain,
The cause of the heartache,
The one that's insane,
I am the bad weather,
The bringer of death,
The eve of forever,
The choker of breath.

Donna Kane

LUCKY FLUKE

In the darkness of the night.
Cases packed, roof rack stacked.
Holiday brought to an abrupt end.
Unaware of the eruption about to unfold.
How had life turned upside down?
Trepidation over hospital stay.
Husband and son standing at my side.
Agonizing pain squeezing every breath,
From my body.
Drifting in and out of blackness beyond distress.
Snowstorm shaker holds bewilderment and weakness.
Pandemonium runs through the family.
Deathly sickness washing through my bones.
Time gently repairs recovery.
Identity grows into a new direction.
Stumbling block demolished from before.

Sharron Hollingsworth

HUSH

Hush, hush the wind whispered softly
Why does he slumber deep?
Hush, hush, the leaves rustled gently
Why can't we wake him from his sleep?
The wind blew a while then quietly said
The soldier dreams in liquid red
And not even we can wake the dead
Hush
Hush.

A Barrett

BULLYING

I did not go to school today,
I may not go tomorrow,
My life is full of sorrow,
I'm being bullied.

I cried myself to sleep last night,
I'll do the same tonight.
I sometimes wake up in the night.
I'm being bullied.

My mum she cried with me last night,
She can't believe it's true,
'I am, I am, I am' I cry,
I'm being bullied.

Their presence there makes me a wreck,
As I go on my way,
They do not care how much they hurt,
I'm being bullied.

I want to end my life today,
And free myself from hell,
I just need someone I can tell,
I'm being bullied.

I wish that I could stand tall and proud,
And look them in the eye,
To show them all that I don't care,
I'm being bullied.

But it's so hard to laugh and smile,
And get on with my life.
I need to shout, and make myself heard,
I am being bullied.

David Townend

CASTAWAY

Beneath my coco-palm I sat alone,
My shoulders bowed beneath the sword of noon;
My driftwood beacon, ready, lay to hand,
Aloft my flag hung wilting in the heat.
With glaring eyes I scanned
The polished shield of ocean and the sky.

Through the mirage sailed the phantom fleet:
I raised no cry,
I did not rise to greet
Each new delusion as she crossed the reef.
But when your raft came sidling through the surf
I stumbled down the blinding beach to meet
You and to haul
The wreckage up the safety of the strand.

I bore you in my arms into the shade
And lying now beneath the tropic night
My prayer is that no ship may ever call.

Geoff Roberts

BRIGHT WHITE HORSES

Bright white horses charging with might,
Hairy coats flowing, swift in flight,
Hurrying, pressing, whiteness growing.
Dark horses left of them, neighing,
Pushing, battling, swerving with spite.

Black winning, darkly as night.
Whiteness gaining, growing in height,
They are stronger, fitter, glowing
       Bright white horses.

Black horses shrinking, determined to fight,
Swerving, battling, pushing the right.
Darkness going, fading, crumbling.
Light overwhelming, tranquillity reigning.
Calm triumphant, only now in sight,
       Bright white horses.

Betty Broom

THE DAY OF THE DEAD MOON
(Isandlwana)

I listened to his telling of the battle,
Enthralled, as he wove his story's web
Of endurance beyond human cognisance,
Courage amidst fear, of desolation
On a pitiless, rock-strewn hill.

I heard the story of my country unfold
Touching me with its pain,
Stirring such deep sadness,
That from the bottom of my soul
I wanted to cry.

I wanted to cry for that beloved country,
The futility and arrogance of war,
For brave men each facing lonely death,
Yet not alone, heaped together, lifeless,
Under scorching African skies.

I needed you to disentangle emotions
That surfaced, intense and unbidden
Suddenly released by tears.
I looked for you,
But you were gone.

Alone, that dark, wet, night
Overwhelmed by my own realities
I wept,
For their world and ours
Until my heart was empty.

Judith James

THE HOUSES OF PARLIAMENT

She is tight-lipped,
Like an assumption,
She trades lives in Ecuador.

The opinions she squanders
Like pearls cast before swine,
She deals treacherously.

The central nucleus, vibrates within
The theme of bamboozle,
Bored with her adornments.

Each persona content of status,
Could suppose to propose,
Downfall, to the man who will not take her hand.

She bathes in prejudice,
And keeps clean her guilt in poverty,
Keeps the secret within her skin.

She hoards belief in purpose,
To say life has no gift or sacrifice,
Except its debts to her universe.

Then takes she her title,
Like a martyr, slightly undefined,
In her luxury and exploit.

Her children born of horses,
Make power, to perpetuate the engine,
And tame justification.

No more hours in the day
Could ever reward you,
With her prosperity.

Kerri Moore

UNTITLED

Where time slowed then stopped
All distance forgotten
There we were
Motionless and dumb
Clinging naked to ourselves
Curiously sexless
The fragrant earth
Damp beneath our feet
Beneath hemlocks' weary shade
Where our futures lay silent
Where the loons recite prehistory
Ripping through the silence of America
Where your pearly opalescent wolves
Endure their horizons
Recite their depths
Recite my doomed mantra
My dead litany

Lone grackle floats black
Above the wildwood
Into October's sky
Maniacally upwards
A beaded yellow eye
Defying gravity
And life and death
All the world's blood
Condensed to an iris
A cold reproachful stare

Chris Lodge

DEAD HOURS

In those dead hours
between night and day
gather yourself into yourself
slip blank between white sheets
disturb no one
quiet enough
hear your breath drawn in

the whispered conversations that die through the wall
paralyse your imagination
again its work is lost
disturb no one
your breath
drawn in
so sudden

whisper your confessions to the dark
because anywhere
there is no one to listen
falling dead into the dark
it's a need to believe
they fall somewhere
that they are with someone

Neil Foggin

THE RAGING SEA

As she sailed through the misty waters
With the sun striking her boughs
I could hear the mournful cries of seagulls
Above the hidden treasures
In the depths of the raging sea
The haunting winds echoing
Laments to whales as they bounced
On leaping muddy white waves
Porpoises dancing near the starboard
Dark aquamarine shadows
Lurking in the hems of the surf
As it surges towards the rocky shore
Seaweed shells and slime
Coral pebbles dirt and grime
Lilac tinged streaks of rain
Falling onto the main

Ann Copland

The Picture Is Complete

The picture is complete, the two sides join
Two halves of different worlds combine
Bringing opposition - unity of vision - not mind

White turns to black and says
'I will love you till the end of time'
And black thinks, 'At last happiness is mine'

The two are one and seem as a whole
Yet emptiness resides within the soul
That which you do not own, you cannot attain
Acquisition is a blind man's game
Pursuit of happiness an unskilful art
Remain at one amidst the heart

Light and shade, both which are true
Brings no ease to either, in a parallax view
No grey occurs in two perfected states,
Division never does relate
And so they stay in wedded bliss
The two not one of separateness

Jennifer Cook

CRYING WOLF

Don't cry wolf too often
my big daddy said,
his claws across my mouth,
and I grew quite.

I remember the woods
of childhood:
white trees and shadowed
patches of thin grass.
No birds,
a pale oblique sun,
and always somewhere
the delicious tang of fear:
where is Mr Wolf?

At school,
auditioned for
Red Riding Hood,
I swallowed my voice entire
and was deemed
no good.
Relegated to the choir
of skipping woodland flowers,
I watched the girl in red
traverse the polished gulf
of parquet
to where Wolfy stood:
a tall boy,
furred of head,
white-fanged.

Years later
in another wood,
you caught me by my
elbow unawares.
Your pelt was silver,
my lips and boots were red.
The proffered paw of
friendship suddenly
swore love.

Running, running to elude
my fear
the forest slewed before me:
no one there.
The cry I heard was
wolfish,
the cottage derelict:
no car nor phone.
Weeping I fell against
the splintered door.
The message, clawed, read
Mrs Wolf come home.

Nancy Cass

RED TAPE

In desperation and trepidation,
The formulation of federation,
Used calculation and formulation
To Arbitration for correlation.

After documentation and deliberation.
The consideration for termination.
In determination the affiliation,
Made remuneration and supplication,
To close early for Wednesdays.

Pat Derbyshire

JANUARY NIGHT IN DEAL

Sea mist descends
her fragile screen.
Filled with the scent
of sea breeze.
Lulling our senses,
and shading our sight.

Burning softly, the moon
lays down his candlelight,
like a dark diamond in the night.
Lending his shadow to twilight
inside smoky quartz skies.
Lulling night, like a lullaby,
as the sea seeps into the sky.

Night fishermen, line the pier,
their lanterns, lulling their fears.
As haunting visions draw near,
sailing high on salty, swelling-breezes.
Then like a sigh, they're lost at sea.
And everything is as it should be.
As the waves, rise and fall,
kissing the sea wall.
And the sky falls into the sea.

Shirley Kelleher

SPIRITUAL CROSSROADS

Are you converting to belief in the impersonal god?
Well, I know you can't truly believe that trash
And neither do I, so let's get out of dodge.
This game is bad misrepresentation of the
Real life that has gone lost.
Life is a vague and constant reminder that
Time will conclude everything we see:
Revelation.
Touch glamour with a velvet-gloved hand and
Move away; don't let it soil your clean mind
Or turn it red: contamination. You are
Full of questions which you say have no answers.
Tell me, how hard have you looked and where?
And are you sincere, or do you think
You're better off in blissful ignorance?
Subordination.
Fold your hands; close your eyes; let your lips
Move in static: Prayer has a power you've not learned to reckon with.
Your tongue is thirsty; your mind stays as busy
As the street signs and screens vieing for divided attention
In garishly meaningless Times Square.
Temptation.
Your bluff is up - how long can you
Keep up this surface pretension
Before you're stripped of your flashy dignity?
Isolation.
Can't you comprehend the beckoning of the spiritual?
The call of the true God is in your very throat
Constricted by your stubbornly misplaced
Allegiance to a dying world of indifference.
Devastation.

It's spelled out on the proverbial wall: there is
Something beyond yourself - God is very personal
And He's outstretched his arm to grasp your hand.
Are you frightened of deeper meanings or will you take it?
Liberation.

Amy Nicole McDougal

DEALING WITH THE SEA

Dealing with the sea
And the weather now
Almost all the time.
And the sea is in the weather pictures
And the weather is in the sea pictures.

Really contending with emotions
Situations and feelings
Usually at the most introspective
With darkened air
And rainclouds above.

Amazed to see gulls and sea birds
Lining up on the shore
Following contours of its structure
Light hard and strange, almost surreal.

Am nevertheless though still concerned
With an inner and outer turbulence.

Work has become abstract enough.

David Hazlett

ROSES IN JUNE

A broken spirit and a contrite heart, God will not despise.
Her heart drowned her soul and her echoing cries filled the air,
yet not a sound was heard.
Her sobs racked her body and could not escape -
they were locked inside. The ever-closed doors to her heart.
Her favourite melodies rang in her ears, yet remained unheard.
Her laughter rippled like a stream but could not flow.
Her words, her sentences of sad and joy were carried away
by the howling of the wind and were blown away,
till not a sound of the wind could be heard,
for the wind was dying down.
Her secret whispers filled her room at night,
as she talked to her one and only friend, her Lord,
in the unseen world around her.
The bird in a gilded cage, which was now beginning to rust from age,
it could not escape,
for the door was locked and the key could not be found.
How she yearned to spread her wings and fly once more,
through the trees, the woods, the hills, around the flowers,
watching the sunlight, the moon and the stars in the sky.
How she longed to be free,
as free as the wind that blew through her hair,
as she warily walked around for winter was now drawing nigh,
but in her heart a memory remained forever,
her summer and her roses in June.

Nicky Young

SNAKE

This true story I do undertake
is to tell you the tale of an angry snake.
As I was digging in a Devon bank
to plant a daffodil
I thought I heard a hissing sound
Quite loud

and sharp
and shrill.

Peering closely at the ground
to try and trace the angry sound.
A snake's head I nearly kissed!
The startled snake stared at me
and hissed.
As I felt ready to take flight,
the grass snake slid smoothly
out of sight
into the woods of dappled light.

Kathleen Harper

A POEM OF CONDOLENCE

I was on holiday in America of that fateful day on Wednesday 9.11.01.
 My cousin woke me and spoke, what he said, made me
feel quite numb, I could not speak, and I was so dumb.
 It was on TV. I went to see, the horror and destruction
that was there, it was too much for anyone to bear.
 The first plane that crashed the tower, the debris
flew in the wind like the petals of a lovely flower.
 Of the people that were there, and of the murderers
who could not care, again the people must have been
 so distraught, the murderers not a thought.
Of the families who are left behind of
 death and destruction they have sought.
What is to be done of this mass murder,
 plunder, and explosions that sounds like thunder?
As I saw the second plane that came into view
 headlong into the tower it flew, again death
and destruction that was there, it was again too much
                                    for anyone to bear.
 The emergency services were so brave and worked so hard,
how I admired them as they played their card.
 Again the people in the street death, dust and
destruction came to their feet.
 As they looked round them in pain and despair,
and wonder how soon the damage would repair.
 Of what has happened! I cannot believe
of these murderers who are so unkind and I
 wonder what next in their mind?
And of these people who did survive, their
 thoughts of their loved ones who are not alive.
And may their souls rest in everlasting peace.

Peter Antonian

REALITY

Zigzagging through the crowds
Of silent laughter and normality
Invisible to capriciousness
That they project.
I tell myself
    I'm normal.
That I'm happy joyous and liberated.
    But that's reality.

In my world of shadows
Torments and tears
Reality is only a delusion.
I try to grasp hold of this
    Thing called joy

It doesn't follow . . .
Or flow through me.
    Am I alive?

B Walker

THE ATTIC

Up the creaky stairs, the attic door.
Children who know where the key is kept
rummage through all the treasures there.
Pictures, tea chests and jewelled gowns.
A sewing machine, a tailor's dummy.
A one-eyed teddy in drunken pose.
Best the battered theatrical skip.
Full of wonders, some fun, some drear.
Photos. Relations in their Sunday best,
stand stiff against the drapes and palms.
An opera hat and a long black cloak
lined in red, that once a villain wore.
Programmes and posters from far-off places
Madras, Hong King, Delhi and Rangoon.
Wigs and make-up, Leichner number five.
Music from failed auditions.
A mandolin, we all tried to play.
Reflections in the cheval mirror
of grotesque little clowns in costumes.
Spectres of the theatre, ghosts from the past.

John J Allan

ABORTION

A family is torn,
the foetus unborn.
Sue fights her emotion,
in thoughts of abortion.

To live is its right,
a fuse I ignite.
But there is still a choice,
says Sue's uncertain voice.

Susan and I had gone to war.
A maelstrom of grief had left its scar.
But throughout the turmoil,
our love didn't cease.
Maybe that is the answer,
the lone road to peace.

Rick Whiteside

AFTER WATCHING THE HIGHLAND ADVENTURE IN SCOTLAND ON TV

It reminded me of my past
Of climbing up Wales's *Snowdon* in a line
What a hard slog but an achievement! so vast
Then we walked down by the rail track.

Another time I climbed up Goat Fell
On the Isle of *Arran*
Coming down I took a turn to the left
And had to keep cool to righten this fact
And get back on my bum to the right path!

I was so lucky! then,
It was after my 15th birthday, ya ken!
I rode down Heathcote Street on my bike
Then rode to Poolys Foundry and then went home
Later I rode down Cob Moor on my bike
And rode back along Wagon Rode

It was thrilling and so fast
It was joy these things from my past!

Marie Barker

CHANGING WIND

Blow wind blow, and open up my mind.
I'm changing now, before me, and behind.
Lies a new road, and the ruins of a world.
A desolate wasteland, and a paradise unfurled.

Wind in my face, will open up my eyes.
Hear my own silence, heed another's cries.
I'm standing tall now, not a stoop or a crease.
Make my own way now, and make my own peace.

You're not a stranger, I'm not estranged.
My mind is clear now, arranged, not deranged.
My thoughts are focused, given up the chase.
Know what I'm here for, my heart is in place.

Blow gentle breeze, to start me on my way.
Off to tomorrow now, I'm done with yesterday.
I guess I know now, the limits of my range.
So blow changing wind, and help me make the change.

R J Ansell

AM A NO A LUCKY MAN?

Am on the wey tae makin cash;
a've solved the problem brawly.
Heretofore or up tae nou
a've suffered a life-time's folly!
A've peyed ma tax - ma income tax
an grudged them every penny.
They've taen it aa, withoot a blink -
am ane, jist ane, amang the many.
But nou, a'll tell ye, for a chynge
we wark it oot oorsel -
a rale obleegin set o fowk
tae me - ane o thur personnel.
It's twa year syne they signed me on;
twa year an each a bonus.
They've sent me back a fortune lads,
a fortune holus bolus!
They're a lovely bunch o braw-like lads
ta'en up wi daen guid
an am a gratefu freen o theirs -
makkin cash daein what am bid!

Andrew A Duncan

THE RAINBOW'S END

One day I wandered in the fields where cows
Were ambling, lying, munching, watching
Me with great brown eyes as I walked on.

Rain had fallen, and the grass was emerald
Where the sun shone down through scattered clouds
And freed the sky to leave it bright.

Fringing near, the wood was silent.
Living creatures, all unseen, were watching there,
Arrested, furtive - only I was moving,
And mushrooms sprouting in fantastic space.

There I found a little man, a small remainder of a dream
Of infancy, unextirpated by the adult throng, he sang
A song no louder than the bluebells would
If all their stamens turned to tongues
And they were shaken in the wind
To sound a splendid carillon. And as he sang
He stroked a caterpillar by his side
As one would strike a cat.

'O I have seen a kitten laugh
And many a cat beside;
And I have seen men full of wrath
To think they did deride!
O I have seen the spider's web
Decked out with pearly dew,
And I have seen a pretty maid
Weep tears that she was not so too!
But I have never yet been by
When men have found the rainbow's end.'

I passed him there. But looking back I saw
The rainbow's foot where he had been.

Joe Smedley

MY ANGEL TEDDY BEAR

Bluebells of May, how can I convey?
The inspiration, hope and love, how do I say?
How do I convey the thankfulness I feel;

Like the shining candle light in the
depths of night. Always there, showing
immense care. My angel teddy bear.

You are truly just like my angel teddy bear.

Tracey Davies

FLY ON THE WALL

O neighbours of a prying kind.
I know thee listen must
especially into my hidden retreat confined.

Yea, ears of magnitude that stretch through walls
be it to my land that once held privacy grand.
Behold! every facet open for thee to make a stand.

O fly on the wall, which I compare thee to.
Wilt thee leave room and join air traffic of gossip
yea of a kind which ne'er be true?

With all surreptitious vehemence
art thee to continue this through and expect gain?
Woe to thy insidious plans that reputation stain.

Beware lest spiders out there catch thee in their web.
Killing fly and stopping disease say I is a must.
Yea, leave gossip alone and replace with trust.

Goodbye neighbour who cannot listen in anymore.
Welcome freedom and privacy
and stay they must behind closed door.

A J Lowe

FREEDOM

Freedom
Free
From pressure
Unbearing feelings
Such as this

I want it all away
Away away with
You

Not wanting
Anymore
Enough is enough
Free

That is what I want

C Osborne

THE EDGE OF TIME
(Millennium Disasters)

So suddenly sleep came,
drenched thoughts gasped,
the flames of life sank
cold . . . their spirits rose
to meet another world
beyond the edge of Time.

How swift the hurricane
blew battered brains
awash, the pulse of life
withdrew . . . peace unfurled
to greet another world
beyond the edge of Time.

With arrow-speed to earth
hearts plunged, nerves
jarred, and charred shells
fell . . . their pearls shone
through another world
beyond the edge of Time.

Crust cracked wide beneath
unbalanced limbs,
split the weight of flesh
agape . . . the inner lights
lit in another world
beyond the edge of Time.

The slumbering giant awoke,
lava-laden violence
choked, ash-blinded bodies
burned . . . the gold within
blazed in another world
beyond the edge of Time.

Evelyn Leite

BOLT

To progress the quest,
It's difficult being robotic,
Go live with the mad instead,
Make the 'Hero's Journey',
Rest on the Isle of the Dead.

My first-met friend,
Offered only hospitality,
Then tried to eat me,
For his tea.

My second met friend,
Ate neither lunch nor tea,
Just a lighter with a battery,
(Instead).

My third-met friend,
Invisibly spoke,
In the silence before dawn,
Inviting me to his wedding,
With Kylie Minogue.

I turned and left,
Retrieving the thing,
I came here to collect,
That being . . .
A lost part of me.

Borsdane

GATTON PARK

A pocket of rural history;
Resting quietly on a hill,
Holds for me a fondness,
That remains within me still.

Climbing the hill from Rocky Lane,
Wellingtonia's stand proud on the brow
They always filled me with such awe,
Yet keep my fascination now.

The Hall built on the skyline,
Is seen from miles around,
With its giant fluted columns.
Imposing and profound

The meadows down by the sparkling lake,
Where fat ponies used to graze,
Remind me now of summers past,
And many happy days.

The tiny part Norman St Andrews Church,
Set among the green of ageing yews,
Still keeps its congregation
And seats upon its pews

Past the school and chapel,
There's a little stony track,
That will lead you onto Horseshoe Wood,
Where we used to hack.

I pause for a while and take a breath,
Then my memory overwhelms,
No longer can I glimpse the lake,
Through clumps of stately elms.

We picked bluebells here in horseshoe wood
Beneath a canopy of ancient beeches,
We'd walk on up to Reigate Hill,
To the woodland's furthest reaches.

June Worsell

WE'RE BACK

A celebrity deathlist privately published
confused and astonished the Cromwellian many
they did not see the return of the few
but they felt their breath and the music
beat like voodoo drums upon their souls
designer numb.
'We're back' said the children of the future
'We come again to claim our inheritance.'
They ran to the suburbs, they hid in their jobs
but the thirst for their blood would not
be slaked by their gradual stepping aside.
The children of the future wanted
only to kiss you, to see you immune
in a poisoned Eaden.
But you laughed and you laughed
and you . . . laughed . . . so you had to die.

Michael Sharron Palmer

REFLECTIVE WINDOWS

Some yellow flowers come suddenly
                at half past seven
Knocking on the breeze,
        so my windows go for me
Find what it is
        this time of night they're wanting
And if they've something
        they want me to see

Their yellow heads
        the frame's interrogating
My curtains wide,
        the panes too take a share
The clock, the couch
        some pieces of the bookcase go outside
To ask the flowers
        what they are doing there

The yellow callers go
        without our learning
Why it was
        they suddenly sought me
And faced reflective windows
        and the room they took along
To enquire what
        they wanted me to see.

Peter Asher

NATURE'S WAY

If I am chosen
to have his baby
then I am his -
he will cherish
his helpmate lady
love and kiss -

Together we'll walk
in Nature's Way
making a peaceful earth
our day to day -
existence will thrive
and I will stay -
His Lady!

How cold - how 'clinical'
the motherless child -
the Donor Baby!

Mary Skelton

ILLUSIONS

Here stands the lamb in Wolven clothing
A claim so sweet you'd like to stake it,
The shrug, the laugh, the carefree smile,
It's so easy now to fake it.
Heart as warm as a summer breeze,
Yet so cold and hard you cannot break it,
The lion's roar, the kitten's trembling,
- Don't jump, my friend, you'll never make it . . .
And still the fire burns inside,
While there's a chance you'll always take it,
In fantasies, sweet love lies cradled,
The dream sleeps on, don't try to wake it.
When fairytales end and life begins,
The path is clear, you can't mistake it,
The wife, the mother, friend and lover
The woman, the child whose tears forsake it.

Michele Amos

HOURGLASS

In the past you returned too many times
to memories, haunted by fear and guilt.
Now things are different;
no longer a victim,
when the clocks go back
the darkness is a warm embrace.
Yes, turn the wooden frame of the hourglass;
you can retrace your steps with confidence;
despite sadness
the present is where you live.

Peter Day

THE ONE THAT GOT AWAY

He tried his hand at the diggings
Up South Central Queensland way
But opals are hard to come by
And he had a thirst all day

A shattered shadow of his former self
He staggered to the bar
Half a dozen stubbies, now he said
Or you won't get very far

The barman grabbed him by the hair
And forced his head to the counter
'Let's have no more of this' he said
'Or I'll send for Maud my daughter'

The man's face paled as he gripped the bar
He knew Maud's reputation
She ate men up and spat them out
With the greatest satisfaction

He turned to go and reached the door
Which burst in right on cue
It hit him with explosive force
It was the last he knew

A shelagh filled the doorway
All six foot six of her
With muscles rippling everywhere
She saw he didn't stir

Then with one hand she picked him up
But he had naught to say
She knew then she had lost this one
The one that got away.

A Marten

I MAY FALL

Hold me by one hand a while longer
Pour your strength in me
Secure stability

Encircled by your arm I am stronger
Sheltered from doubt
Taking a way out

Unsteady, unsure of each movement
Each step made with care
Away from despair

Watch me closely for any improvement
Releasing your hold
Becoming more bold

Taking steps unsupported at last
Stay close by my side
Without your guide

I may fall

Patricia Toulson

RUSH HOUR

Under the cover of darkness
a newspaper stand's an out of town home
the humdrum nexus of morning,
fills with destitution, as stars go out.

A walk by the river
picks-up caricatures and peace
made for flesh and steel some hours ago
like slaves at their master's feet.

Take them up in a palm, these fugitive organs,
tangled round weed and mortar,
catch them from a viaduct, dead headed,
weaving through the city.

Ian Bishop

SUBMISSIONS INVITED
SOMETHING FOR EVERYONE

POETRY NOW 2002 - Any subject,
any style, any time.

WOMENSWORDS 2002 - Strictly women,
have your say the female way!

STRONGWORDS 2002 - Warning!
Age restriction, must be between 16-24,
opinionated and have strong views.
(Not for the faint-hearted)

All poems no longer than 30 lines.
Always welcome! No fee!
Cash Prizes to be won!

Mark your envelope (eg *Poetry Now) 2002*
Send to:
Forward Press Ltd
Remus House, Coltsfoot Drive,
Peterborough, PE2 9JX

**OVER £10,000 POETRY PRIZES
TO BE WON!**

Judging will take place in October 2002